TITLE PAGE

Poems and Other Scratchings

BY

A. Barth

Trafford Publishing

Printed in Victoria, Canada

National Library of Canada Cataloguing in Publication

Barth, A.
      Title page / A. Barth.
ISBN 1-55395-719-9
     I. Title.
PS3602.A767T47 2003   811'.6   C2003-900661-1

TRAFFORD

This book was published *on-demand* in cooperation with Trafford Publishing. On-demand publishing is a unique process and service of making a book available for retail sale to the public taking advantage of on-demand manufacturing and Internet marketing. **On-demand publishing** includes promotions, retail sales, manufacturing, order fulfilment, accounting and collecting royalties on behalf of the author.

Suite 6E, 2333 Government St., Victoria, B.C. V8T 4P4, CANADA

Phone	250-383-6864	Toll-free	1-888-232-4444 (Canada & US)
Fax	250-383-6804	E-mail	sales@trafford.com
Web site	www.trafford.com	TRAFFORD PUBLISHING IS A DIVISION OF TRAFFORD HOLDINGS LTD.
Trafford Catalogue #03-0082		www.trafford.com/robots/03-0082.html	

10   9   8   7   6   5   4   3   2

In loving memory of my brother Brad
who embraced life with such passion and strength.

When you looked at that hurdle,
after they raised it one notch higher,
where did you find the courage
to run, full steam, right at it
and sail right over it?

List of Poems by Page Number

cont'd. . . . .

cont'd . . . .

A warning to
the faint of heart,
bring with you the light
if you fear the dark.

And for those of you
who've squandered your youth,
within you may find
a bit of truth.

On the Wings of Hope

Soaring high above the trees
was I
Caring not of the land
as it blurred by
Dive and dip
hither and toe
Floating gently
to and fro
Feel the breeze
caress my feathers
Extend
Contract
Circle back

Trial and heir

Each one, us all,
born with heart and brain.
In the beginning,
we all are the same.
Then hit-
SMACK
-with societies hand,
gasp our first breath of life,
amongst this strange man.
Some raised with kindness,
some with despair.
One grows to judge,
one learns to care.
Some decide to turn a cheek,
or blame their misfortunes
on the mild and meek.
For others, life
is merely a game.
Each peg they slot
brings fortune and fame.
We spend our lives
divided as such.
Some with too little,
some with too much.
Yet in the end
we all pass the same.
We're judged by our hearts,
and not by our brains.

Mother Ocean

In awe we stand before you,
the perfect combination.
Such power and tenderness,
with every wave formation.

With calming reassurance,
you guide the frightened barge.
And never can a man forget,
the Lady is in charge.

Battles fought upon your lap,
many sailors washed to sea.
And through the ages as you wept,
many people you set free.

So grand is your past,
touching every nation.
Only with respect we treat,
My Lady, God's creation.

Nothing is for naught

I knew a little girl
who wanted to become a soldier,
a ballerina, a wrestler, an artist,
a poet, and a mother.
She became a soldier,
now she has discipline.
She became a ballerina,
now she has balance and coordination.
She became a wrestler,
now she knows the strength of her opponent.
She became an artist,
now she knows the beauty of creation.
She became a poet,
now she knows the power of words.
She became a mother,
now she knows the importance
of a little girl.

Relevancy

One voice with
constant flat's
going up.
Scribbles in my mind
then scratches to go
out the other side.
More voices fill the
cafe, it's lunch time.
Why should they be
concerned with my silence?
Public places mix the
batter, the slop, of
every voice in the city.
Lips flapping over teeth
only aware for one moment
when food is stuffed
through, or
they sneeze and
bite their tongue.

The ponds of imagination

Some are shallow
some are deep,
what is the source
of the thoughts we keep?

A rushing river
or a trickling creek,
it's plain to all
as soon as you speak.

Glacier dug
with power and force,
a strong minded man
consider the source.
Where a cold, steel tractor
sat scooping the ground,
there a stagnant mind
will always be found.

Just as a mountain
can be moved or left still,
the depth of a mind
is the heart of man's will.

Listen

Bandwagons full of empty applause
pioneering new dimensions.
For every effect there is a cause
creating distrust and tension.

We elbow our way through history
competing against the past.
Yet like our fathers we fail to see
the covenant that lasts.

Wailing our crimes against all others
for acts we know are wrong.
We bleed and debauch our brothers
while singing the same song.

Internal fights and hardened scorn
give birth to lasting hate.
A land whose ground is truly torn
will eat from Satan's plate.

Don't feed upon this infected worm
lest you become a stone.
Hold your faith and troth so firm
the truth becomes your own.

Zephyr

Just then   the wind shifted
and you were there
           I thought
      for sure   I saw you   smelled
your fragrance
           captured your wave
                in a shuffle of leaves
                                    ducked
under a branch   and turned
           you were gone
called your name
      around cliffs   and under rocks
begged the wind to change again
and yet
                I know you were here
      you were
                here
                weren't you!

Mean Ships Sink

Never get angry
at angry people.
Don't cut your tongue
to match their challenge.
If you pimple
your personality
with deep pores
of hate and anger,
you could permanently
scar your spirit.
Never reflect their image.
They will never see the good
if you bed with them.
Allow their hurt
proper time to heal
until want becomes
wallow,
then
give prayers at a hearts distance.
For those who want
to remain
in anger
you, alone, can do nothing.
Sad to watch them
sink in stink.
Sadder still
if you follow.

Garden of Strength

Come to the garden
where we remain free,
come and sit
listen to me
and us.
Halt your breath
control your tongue,
listen
and silence is song.
Without a word
beauty is spoken,
natural quiet
reveals life's truths
and awakens
a sense within us all.
Seldom we pause
to be aware
of the strength
we gain
in the Garden.

Wisdom

These tears I cry;
Blood, sweat and years.
Whose life do I really mourn,
those gone
or my present fears?
I thought with age
came wisdom.
Seems I can only regress.
As my life rumbles forward,
more and more I repress.
A shallow cesspool belches toxins,
the deep one only quakes.
Dug from years of misery,
it has learned from its mistakes.

From the beginning, there was the end.
A doom-sayer I am not!
But why, I wonder, must I travel so far,
to get to this very same spot?

For J.S.O.

You.
You stole my heart.
And for what?
Are you now a better man?
So much greater in your mind's eye
since your worthless half
has been expelled.
Now you're free of ignorant me
with the time to pursue
your beloved degree.
By now, book knowledge
is bursting your brain,
though I doubt
common sense has any domain.
You called me cute
and thought I was simple
like a pet to eventually slaughter.
You couldn't see beyond yourself
so how could you see me?
Don't you know
I loved you still,
without a P.H.D.
My world to you
was petty and small
which you confirmed
since I wouldn't crawl
up the length of your pedestal.

I loved the man
who loved me then,
without a promise of greatness.
Had you not changed
to fit the family mold,
I would love you still.
You.

Imprisoned Distance

We speak in canopied sentences,
no doubt we are aware.
Our eyes hold up
the chains you see
for the key we can not share.

Tribulation, '92

Swirl, swirl
the undertow.
Grabbing, twisting
tossed.
Here I am
then
there I go.
My personal holocaust.

Study your steps,
each print you leave.
Did you impress
the thread you weave?

Whitewash

Even as the sun repented,
there was beauty.
I couldn't   for the life of me
            nor the moment
take my eyes from dreary haze
caught up in the white
particles falling   then parallel
there they went   coming at me
some must be reaching destiny
the black plow banks are turning
only speckled spots   of ugly
remain   windshields   black street coated
coating   caught underneath
the beauty   purifier of the
accumulated grunge   the wind
washed white   drifted dunes grow
again the city suckles
the breast of
Mother Snow.

I Love My Shelf

Before I knew it
I wasn't myself.
Same face and hair
now my stomach's a shelf.
You see the obvious,
one grows from within.
What you cannot perceive
is how I became thin.
The weight of my child
stretched more than my tummy
who is this person
that thinks spinach is yummy?
I once knew my thoughts
and was quick on my feet
now some stranger controls
my every heart beat.
how bizarre to become
unknown to myself,
though I'll be glad when it's over
I love my shelf.

Color crayons

Color crayons and felt pictures.

Kindergarten rooms.

Just weaned from Johnson's baby lotion,

barely left the womb.

So quick to wear the make-up,

and act like Mom and Dad.

Too soon they'll learn the hardship,

and realize what they had.

The Grocer

My Mom and Pop
they said, "get a life".
So I went to the grocer
and bought me a wife.
We built a house
a home we did
went back to the grocer
and bought us a kid.
So thrilled with our baby
we thought for a score
then went back to the grocer
and bought a few more.
Now my Mom and Pop,
they enjoy my life.
I think they may even
enjoy my wife.
The grocer, he's a very rich guy
and though I haven't a penny
he's no richer than I.

There are cats creeping in my walls
and redneck junkies down the hall
with three birds in a cage in their
kitchen. I call this home!
Burnt toast and cigarette smoke
greet me in the morning, that and
wailing water pipes. I *do* have a room
with a view- a good view. One would
think it a "landmark" view for what
I pay. It's fine for me though,
generally quiet. Big enough to house
my virtues and humble enough to
constrain my doubts. Had I more money,
I'd get a bigger place, but then
I'd have to sacrifice the creeping cats
and character. I wonder, some days,
just how productive I would be with
enough money to take the rest of my
life off. Would I still grumble
at burnt toast and wailing pipes, or
would I condemn the place, tear it down,
build a parking lot with a view
and charge redneck junkies to come
and bird-watch? How tall would I have
to build the walls to house my expensive
virtues? And could there be enough
mortar to constrain my doubts,
would "humble" even have a place?

9 * 1 * 1

Right through me
they scream.
Like a ghoulish dream!
Pain and suffering
their destination.
A rythmic light
taps my window at night.
And red the perfect color!

How many times can one divide a heart and
still keep it soft and pliable? How many times
can a person send a piece of their heart out
into an unknown world without them, to be taken
care of by a stranger? How strange to have a
little bit everywhere and yet, be left with an
abundance, a seemingly never-ending supply.
I imagine, if one was to take a role of every
piece one has sent away, only then would the
reality be so overwhelming that rigor might set
in and thus the pump to share no more,
turning cold and hard, slamming, if you will,
the bitter door to love no more.
Better not to take count,
rather,
look for more strangers!

Fishing in painful waters

I am not completely comfortable,
not today,   not this week.
Things keep popping up in my day-to-day
relating to specs of my past.
My "bad memory" chamber
is a lonely walk
with dripping walls
resonating in my thoughts,
it's a cold, damp place.
I'd never visit there on purpose.
Yet,
some lives entwine with mine,
repeating the same mental notes
as those that I have locked in my chamber.
Their feelings of pain
seem to call up my ghosts
as their fresh hurt
recognizes my old.
I want to hate them for this
but it's not their fault,
for if I could
rid my own thoughts
of this cold, lonely chamber,
then their dripping pain
would not resonate in me
and I could more freely
help them
with their own fresh hurt
and old ghosts.

Just,

who is
just around the corner,
just in need of a drink,
just in need of the truth,
just a bit underprivileged,
just a bit slow
or lacking self-control.
Who exactly
is Just?
Maybe just
a little spanking
or just a bit
of discipline
or just a hug.
Perhaps justice would prevail
if just a chunk of love
would be given from our
overly protected hearts
and shared with
just a few.
Could we just
slow down enough
to recognize ourselves
and comprehend
that the extent of our existence
is just a touch
of compassion away.

Brain surgery

It takes a calculated eye

perhaps,

to see an instant of time elapse.

It takes a steady hand

I'm sure,

to divide the obvious from obscure.

And a hearty shove is needed

no doubt,

to make a forward turn about.

But the trickiest task to perform

yes, it's true,

is to tell your enemy,

"Hey, I forgive you!"

Don't ever think otherwise

For all the mistakes I've done
and somehow
overcome
every angry day
at you
I most regret.
For all the times we've laughed
at each other
and ourselves,
I take comfort in knowing
every ebb of tide
secures
and redefines
the gift God
gave us both.

With all these theories,
floating around in my head.
About "true living",
and when we are dead.
I heave forth a sigh,
from deep in my chest.
As I wonder if "theories",
should be put to rest.

A pennant before repentance

Feelings left   un-chaperoned
will travel   on   to question
        Shoulders bend
              brows pinched tight
angry,   open-ended thoughts
      unite   and pool
nudging the tongue
        A battle rages
Misconstrue   carries the banner
    silence is first to fall
            wounded
Guilt charges   saber raised
willing to die   for anger
Talk   so cheap   it's traded
        for fuel
Fire scars emotion
The tongue gains power
      blindly   it murders truth
            bloodied lips   forget the kiss
      and stand stern
beside the tongue
Feelings find   that in the end
      the question sought
            turned the river   red
Guilt has captured the banner!

If not once you have felt
that the hand you were dealt
has been useful or even appealing,
why not take a chance
and venture a glance
to find out who's been doing the dealing?

From innocent lies and lullabies

You think my tone too somber
because I abhor the lies
of society   a backwards
people   hiding clean   while
sashaying rags for kings
twisting grotesque wrongs
until they resemble tiny rights
at least to those in retrospect
who deny there was ever defiance
and peddle tracts for Zeus and Zen
sell open minds to foolish men
who dine with deceit and sleep
with her brother   a cursed
child unknowingly born   to generations
laying down roads to hell
          and traveled well
pin brass upon the chests
of cowards   who pollinate
the seeds of hate   and rescue
filth from fire.
You think me too intolerable
because I don't give in to chance
or lottery   or sweepstakes at my door
you praise the eagles watchful eye
yet question the songbirds
lullaby   under constant surveillance
for fraudulent behavior   put the "Press"

on it and try it in the paper
let's air our trials
and hide our poor
in governed shacks   disguised
as community projects   form
committees to keep them down
ship their children out of
town to schools with the greatest
intent   hell bent
on proving the innate good in man
with solar stations   watch
the invisible nuclear trash of foreign
nations   and project peace
through underground cables   labeled
strictly "PG".
Welcome to the melting pot
a sun-baked kettle   of pungent
prejudice   rot   free votes
paid for by tobacco thieves
marionette king in a house
of greed   with guards to keep him there.

Whenever Your hem is upon me

And there came a time
when doubters   fastened
heavy chains on my heart
I questioned my convictions
running with my burdens
to a grave   far from my
Savior
Even so much as I   stumbled
through the field of repent
my eyes further casting shadows
on faith and redemption
Laden in sorrow
I rested in retreat   only for a moment
then I raced to the fire
which was the light
and gave of my grave
to forgiveness and mercy
where I found   the whispers
silent.

Bee

That was the year that changed my life,
forever.
You died and I got married.
It lasted only five years,
my marriage, I mean
you're still dead.
Now I cuddle up with my bowl of
freshly popped, "If I'd only's…"
listening to Hank moan his lonesome oldies.
You were the baby
and you played it well.
Only now are your tantrums heartwarming.
If only you could still throw a Tonka truck
across the sandbox at me
or tutor me in math,
thrice your grade.
You always did have to be first.
Well now you've done it,
you were the first to die.
I should have known marriage in a death year
would never work out.
I never should have married.
You never should have died.

The uglier
we see our reflection
the more hideous
our garments of cover become.

Silver Cocktails and Brandy Bullets

Need you don
fur
and sharpened teeth
to live the
night
of the howling beast?
Cold, piercing rays
of the
midnight sun
at it's fullest
a hollow
one.
Eyes
of fire
your body trembles
a fearsome
creature
it resembles.
When man
becomes
animal
with drunken sin
the clever, dark
host
will let him in.
A lust for madness
and temporal satisfaction

drives the
un-sober wolf
towards fatal attraction.
When white sun falls and
red
ascends
the truth of your
night-kill
reshapes and
blends.
As your
body returns
to daylight
bloodied jowls
hidden in your
sleep
you awake
with the sweat
of lost memory
and the fiery
beast
you keep.

It is Said

It is said that beauty

is only skin deep.

I believe,

it's much deeper than that.

For those whose beauty

is merely a wig,

would do well

to purchase a hat!

When we crawl
we yearn to walk.
And when we walk
we yearn to run.
But when we run
we tire fast.
And wish to crawl
like in the past.

Homework

As rushed as we are
seems little wonder
that our homes
are wayside.
Much laundry time
is saved
on linen,
why wash
what you never live in.
A fine oak table
intended for dining
holds two months
of mail
and climbing.
Electric bill
surprising low
all energy spent
on the go.
We balance to live
within our means
yet twenty-four hours
only seems
enough to pay for half.
When we retire
there's time to laugh.
Whenever that may be,
sixty-two, no, sixty-three.

Ah, heck
let's make it seventy-five.
And if I'm alive,
I'll travel,
I'll show my family love,
I'll be the person I was
before I hugged
my laptop daily planner
and answered my car phone
more than my children.

The grey roof of imagination
is shingled with curiosity.

The Nature of Things

Down the alley

on the right

he yaps

to make up for his height

I guess

and her parrot mocks him

down the alley

to the left

her pet in a cage

on the picnic table.

Yap! Yap!

Baark, Baark, Whaap!

It could be annoying

if it wasn't so funny.

Referencing the Band

My waiter said;
        "All the Deadheads are
        now Fish-heads".
Isn't that funny?
Still heads   either Dead or Fish
I presume   the final chapter
will read   "Dead Fish"
        lost their heads   and found
no water in the channel   no more
trail   to spawn tie-dyed cults
no more   bastard guru's
to lead the chants
        to vault
societal barriers
        to fault
the rich and powerful
with no team to cheer
maybe grass could grow
on their field   possibly life
where the dead have trampled
        little, buzzing, insects
could deposit drops of love
        on every blade
heads will lift   from the field
to sing   and fish may fall
from heaven.

Weather From My Window

There goes a soaked, green person,

staggering past my window.

Green shirt, green pants and galoshes,

it's been raining all day and, you know!

My sidewalk's become a collage,

fallen leaves, sticks and debris.

I watched my yard transform,

from a solid to a sea!

I haven't seen my friendly squirrel,

or any animal, in fact.

Except that green man with galoshes,

wet leaf upon his back.

When space between two lovers, dear,
sparks and spurrs . . . . it sputters too.
Then closeness prevails to close
the gap and once again the lovers
rejoice and hold close one another,
forcing the space out from between them
to form an area around them.
It's no wonder they seem to be residing
in a world outside of ours.

The Play

They belch their boast
as on they go.
So sure and cocky
are the crow.
While these sit cooing
of their love.
The soft and sensitive
turtle dove.

Yonder bounds
the hare so free.
Sucking drops of dew
no care has he.
Cool morning breeze
will flutter by.
To raise and carry
the butterfly.

The flowers bow
the trees applaud.
This heavenly stage
directed by god.
Over the hill
the sirens scream.
The peace destroyed
the slate wiped clean.

Chasing Mother's Rainbow

Flannel pajamas and fuzzy slippers.
Eight little imaginations playing games.
A sleep-over far from slumber.
Innocence hugging unknown fears
and softly kissing eventual tears.
Eve's children debating apples.
On the bedside of dawn
one foot in the rainbow,
heaven appears never-ending.
Frosted ideas of Mother's bliss
only perpetuates the lie.
Every young girl believes in this
embedding the thorn in her eye.
Strong, loose, pigheaded or giving
the world will so define her.
Trading her flannel for silk or rags
the rainbow is only a memory.
And heaven? Wishful thinking?
Now wearing her Mother's fuzzy bliss
in worn out slippers and humbleness,
she plays the hand-me-down game.

Free to return

It shouldn't be
that when we leave the nest,
to return
would feel like a trespass
or regression.
No,
we should feel the love returning
bringing with it
new songs of joy
fresh sprigs for the forest
to keep it rich and vital,
expanding its boundaries
yet connected to the core,
all fitting together in the arms of history,
nurtured by common belief
while contributing examples of life
and love,
every tree abuzz
with the spirit of understanding
and the earnest pursuit of pure joy.
No,
it shouldn't be a regression,
it should be a relief
in a safe haven
on a branch that feels every leaf move
in the whisper of a breeze
or the howl of a storm.

Yes,
it should be a reflection
of the nature of things
as they were
and as they change
all staying, simply the same
in the never ending warmth
of the nest.

Shattered Stability

We sit separately
in a room
we once occupied together.
Awkwardly dividing up memories.
Making final decisions
on what of the past
we will want most to remember
in the future.
"Oh, he was more my friend
and she was yours.
You loved the castles
and I the shores".
Here is a stack
of hard to decides,
the best image
the worst to divide.
Each memory he keeps
cuts a thread of my past.
I'm left with some
to patch together,
to quilt my history anew.
Calm and subdued
we make our choices.
Here a laugh
and there a tear.
We wonder how it came to this.
Shattered stability
face the fear.

Man, all consuming

We go about
and about we go.
Consumes' the only
word we know!
Some of this
and a bunch of these.
Pay no mind
to the trees.
Build your home
on sacred ground.
Throw your refuse
all around.
For we are man
the superior being.
We'll destroy it all-
do you get what
I mean?!?

Life is a new apprenticeship
every day and hard work.

Hickory Horse

High upon a hickory horse
he's an outlaw and a king,
where innocence and fantasy
perform in center ring.

He laughs at grown-up challenge
afar in the distant fields
his youth and play-fullness
form a safe and solid guild.

For now his gentle passion
heaps color on the wind,
a pallet full of adventure
a protected eye from sin.

What subtle circumstances
may fall this happy king,
could he keep his heart so pure
no mournful singers sing?

Pray he forms a great army
all glitter on hickory horse,
a sincere and loving king
learned mercy and remorse.

So many thoughts- work, don't work,
need the hours, need the money, hate
the place! Want a house all mine-
no debt. Want a love all mine- no guilt.
Want a world to house my love, a perfect
world- no fear, no hate, no deceit,
no clocks, no shopping malls.
Only gardens and oceans and birds and
small furry creatures. Warm days, warm
winds, warms smells. Cool nights
when the hero's come home to sup.
Thick quilts to lay them down on
and rub them in oils.
To lie still with them and feel
their rhythm and join their rhythm
and become one in love.

If you share with me
your burden,
then if you should fall,
I will know by what means
to gather you up.

Snare Drum

How odd to be dying.

I felt removed but was very much
in the thick of the present.
This tiny man
drawing closer to himself
and growing.
Last night, he grew so large
in my heart
he spoke, for the first I've heard
of his deep regrets,
his self-condemning guilt.
He shined as he cried.

She gave her life by his side
through hell
and an occasional, sunny window.
She built escapes for herself
he tore them down.
Now he is too weak
to approach her escapes
and she feels guilty to plan,
free from his ranting.
Oh, he can still talk it down
but she knows there will be no more
physical destruction.

What a struggle I witnessed.
Feelings and emotions
being shot at me
as if psychedelic fireworks
aimed at my heart, mind, spirit and soul.
Some popped just outside,
some burst deep,
still others are fizzing
waiting for the right moment to explode.

Without a spoken word
the beat nails you.
It gets caught in your throat,
pulses high electricity through your limbs,
puffs your chest 'til you stand straighter.
It beats so deep in your soul
you know at once
that you are connected
to more than just this body.

It is proud and loud
it fears not.
It will echo true
for we all know the beat,
we are born of it
and we die of it.

Before we know the outcome,
the foot is yet un-shoed.
Our dreams are free to wriggle,
our minds are free to brood.

From an Attic in Duluth

All the way out
to Wisconsin
I see,
a thick blue line
across the lake from me.
In spinning snow
the rooftops seem
as if the shingles
are made of steam.
Blue shadows cast
on shivering lovers
the day a virtual
watercolor.
And I
the power
to ink it out
I draw the shades
of paramount.
Inside these walls
of thick insulation
I paint fluid verse
on alienation.
My teapot sputters
and sounds the alarm
I've missed the daylight
and wasted its charm.

There was brilliant beauty
and a calming hue
yet I chose black and white
with a one-sided view.
Tomorrow
I'll travel
across the bay
I'll stand in Wisconsin
and look back at today.

The Sensual Midnight Snack

Lunge and lust

hard hip thrust

wrench and tear

release the air

Blipity-blip

fill the lip

just to the top

then stop.

Now that you've got your glass of milk,

you're peeved to find

you've left behind

those sinful chocolate cookies!

The Holidays

We give thanks
thanks be given.
When the turkey's all gone
we go on with our livin'.

We go to church
on Christmas day.
We go and sit, and listen and pray.
Then we go home
and go to bed.
"Next Christmas, let's take
a vacation instead".

New Year's comes
resolutions are made.
Though their starting dates
are delayed and delayed.

Every year
we look forward to this,
with dreamy eyes
and visions of bliss.
Maybe the future
will bring forth new ways,
of wishing each other
Happy Holidays!

To the ambitious artist
it's really a treat
to see them all out there
canvassing the streets.

Passing Time with Dict.

For lack of a better center
of gravity
I'll think amongst myself.
Without a model of simple
sanity
pulling Webster off it's shelf.
Words of color
with drab, gray image
produce a laissez faire
of spirit
and attitude.
Am I so fixed amongst myself
that I no longer care,
nor wish to share in
the social art
of pomp and purpose?
Since you don't mind
leaving my devices
to be amongst themselves,
then here I'll sit
in simple mind
passing time
with diction.

Confined to Shadows

Completely alone
on this cot where I lie
talking to the shadow
in the corner of my eye.
I can always form figures
in the cheap, stucco walls
like the ones from my childhood
sculpted by clouds.
I light a Camel
and watch the smoke play
it comes off in a hurry
then slows on it's way
up towards the top
it scatters about
with my hand I lean over
and like a god
snuff it out.
I plan for tomorrow
how I'll dress
what I'll say
I promise myself
not to throw it away.
I make big plans on my cot
confess my transgressions
I even imagine
I have cosmic connections.
Private time is over
a voice yells "lights out".
The striped shadows reveal
what I'm really about.

Grey Zone

As I walked across the parking lot, leaving
work by noon, I reached the exit lift-arms
when I felt it. I looked around, construction
on the aquarium, new pipelines being laid
under the viaduct, under the tracks. Still
so very calm, quiet. Too quiet. My spirit
squirmed, "This isn't right, something's wrong.."
I walked on, coming to the street crossing.
Looking both directions, no traffic as far as I
could see, yet, at the center yellow line, from
the edges of my sight, came a vehicle in each
direction. I crossed in time, but a bit unnerved.
Just then, the wind tumbled a dry leaf and a
discarded take-out cup between my steps. I had
to get home.
No peace at home;
as I sat in the grass, proclaiming that the oil
filter on my mower was in cahoots with the
grey spirit of the day, two birds assailed my
shoulder, missing it as a perch by inches. They
fought in violent bellows until crashing my
raspberry bush. One grasped the upper feather
and
the other took flight.
And, to truly denote the death in my day;
I smelled what I thought was a brush fire on
the hill. Turned out to be my castle burning.

I have a spot, a building from a dream, only
this beauty is of old and neglected age.
I thought I might like to buy it, with a little
love and a lot of attention, her walls would
shine as once before, in truth, I was saving
for that. Tonight it caught and burned.
There is nothing demonic or even horrific in
this story just the hair-raising acknowledgement
of a grey day. I still managed a good
nights sleep.

Statutory Offense

Slinking down the city stink
hellfire between his ears,
they've convinced another unsaved soul
to torment tender years.
Driven by the damned of God
he's sure to make a score,
he destroys her youthful innocence
secure in body no more.
The rabid dog is a drooling beast
not caring who he bites,
mothers protect your children
from the evil he ignites.

As she grows to be a woman
memory firmly intact,
she'll carry that evil filth
and she'll feel that evil act.
Don't ask her why or ask her how
she does the things she does,
she'll pierce your heart with distant eyes
and coldly answer, "Because.."

Because one night a drooling dog
was listening to the flame,
with one swift bite he stole from me
and this is what I became.

Go ahead and paint your wagon
purple, blue or yellow.
No reason you should keep it red
like all the other fellows.

Window Shopping

Once,
while window shopping,
all day drizzle
I was sopping.
The sign read,
"Come on in"
a porcelain goose
with a stupid grin.
A roar and a splash
as the city bus passed,
"they make these walks too narrow!"
On the corner stands
the homeless man,
"Will work for food - God Bless"
She drops him a dime
spare change from lunch,
business jacket in a dress.
Outside the office,
the smoking fella.
Hand in pocket,
home team umbrella.

As the rain
turns to sleet
the rush hour traffic
no doubt will meet
a nasty ride at five.

It's time for me
to head on home,
small apartment
two cats and a sink.
I turn to go
the sleet to snow
and leave the goose with a wink.

Observer in Delivery

From sack of life
and cord like latex
he plunges into existence
This sterile violence
called natural birth
We scream and coo
in awe.

Father leans
to cut the ties
of Mother to her child
Tiny fingers scratch the air
as silence fills his lungs
then cries upon release.

Nurse in mask
wipes, stamps and bundles
His mark is made
Simple comfort ended
Now pleading life begins.

Not Forsaken

Without the light
the man will stumble
for darkness has no map
it intrudes on every
weary front
looking for souls to sap.

So set your compass
to the Son
and walk the road
less taken
May your guiding light
be always bright
knowing you
are not forsaken.

The Missed Among us

I'm no authority
on why death comes
or why it visits
some early.
Why do some abuse life
and stay long
while others barely
catch their breath
before it's taken away?
Which is harder for those left behind;
a quick thunder in the night
with no chance to share goodbye,
or long suffering?

Flowers still bloom
the wind still blows
as if everyone
and nothing
knows
of our personal loss,
our tragedy of the heart,
the wrenching in our soul,
the choice to keep breathing
awkwardly alone.
To search for the power
to embrace joy
without the guilt
of not sharing
happy moments

with the ones
whom death
has taken.
And when we cry out
screaming tears of why,
until our throats as
raw as our emotions,
we are comforted some,
by God
by friends
by time.
Alone at our bedside
we weep,
heaving our shoulders
as tears mix with snot
and we cannot
stop it,
don't want to.
Whose faith can dry the tears,
even more,
stop the inward
waterfall?

Faith, strength and time
all contribute to growth.
Given the years,
even a tree will grow
over a barbed wire fence
set piercing its' bark

at its' waist.
But we can all
clearly see the scar,
the pain of growing around a puncture.
Yet life is set
for death.
Two triumphs we all go through.
And we, the ones
missing the gone,
will eventually
be missed.
And the flowers bloom
and the wind blows.

Sometimes life
is like typing with boxing
gloves.

The thought is there
but the execution
is muddled.

I spent the day building character;

that night I punched the window
I drank my poetry drunk
and threw-up all over my values
It cost me $41.00 for the pane
and a night on the couch
My most poetic line, "I need my space"
as it collapsed around me
With my forehead resting loudly on my tongue
I awoke to the sounds of morning
and the stench of yesterday's verse.

There is empathy
and there is sympathy.
The prejudice heart
knows nothing of either.

Stick To The Freeway

Alive on the streets
of small town mentality
is a shining example
of ignorance gone law.

Incased in a world
of twisted reality
unable to recognize
the cause of the flaw.

Generations shut in
behind bigot doors
with prejudice windows
and cold biased floors.

Much honor and pride
fertilizes this seed
God, country and freedom
for this they will bleed.

An open community
welcoming all of it's kind
come in and find safety
amongst the blind.

To the traveling stranger
I bid you, take heed
a poorly marked exit
could trap you indeed!

It's so very hard to think in a city
during the day. Too much interference
as the force of every man's will rushes
here and there, being known and accounted
for. Having beat the night by no will
of their own, still they stand and chant
and beat their chests as if a warriors
victory they won, and each, they all,
take credit for the sun. Knowing not
the one, who sent them light and not
at all eager to oblige or bend a knee
in thanks. Through the day of whistles,
bells and horns, busily feasting on the
day as if no prior knowledge of the dark.
'Til darkness knocks and lights come on
behind locked doors, bells are silenced,
wills to bed. Warriors, reduced to children
lying hushed through the night, praying
then, for rest and strength to sound the
mighty alarm at dawn. Once again proclaiming
victory to their glory.

Soul Boxes

I was about to say
"I wasted my morning"
Looking back over my years
But if looking back
was a waste of time
how much was wasted
to get here?

A battered blue box
once held my mother's jewels
now a hodge-podge of mine
A shiny wooden box
given to me by the one
who stole my faith
now houses the
remnants of that love.
And books, photos, clippings
Awards, buttons, pins
Old stuff
Eyeglasses of a fifth grader
wristwatches from back
before time was a race
My many hats
cards and letters
Junk.
Junk?

If so,
then the very being
of my character
all the jewels
that have joined to make
me
who I am now
are they garbage?
No
I am the sum total
of all that lies within
the secrets of the things
that I decided to stick
in a box
and waste time
looking back on.

Aaron's Apron

Mother lost her mind that day
the cancer came in
and took him away.

I put on the apron
too short for it's hem
and became their surrogate
no longer their friend
I cooked and cleaned
and helped them through school
an under aged parent
forced to rule
I grew up too fast
with anger and pride
the moment you left us
my innocence died
A little girl
with grown up fears
small, calloused hands
dried momma's tears
As the apron grew smaller
and my siblings reared
my momma controlled
her constant tears
I left on my journey
in search of me
as I tried to forget
the lost sanity.

A mother alone, no children her own
wanting her place of peace
Years of rearing without endearing
formed her pride and hard beliefs.

To this day, a strong stubborn woman
walks with honor, gracefully.
I've now her apron and her calloused hands
alive inside of me.

In rented days of melancholy
stripping stems of want from folly

Fear can motivate concession
to sin   accept the lesser
of two evils   shrugging off
the choice   a zombie voice
will fall in line   converted to
the masses
        marching, marching
chained to the "freedom" of man
exercise restraint and wrestle
faith till death
        too late.
Grey bellied clouds are light
on top   which we see not
        can not
through misty motivation
heavy steps we watch our toes
only lifting our heads to force
fake smiles at other's faces
and looking down our nose
sin stacked on sin
        in thicket woes
a silent voice
retreats to the top of the clouds
safely sitting above grey fear
overlooking our grouped "independence"
and drops a tear   lost in the
river of our ignorance.

The grass is always greener where your neighbor made lemonade.

Sunset at Breezy Point

Stale smoke
and fried food
Fishhooks, toilet paper
and a beer
Pool table, pinball
and electric bowling
Unisex restroom
Tall tales, tall stools
and short order
Peanuts, popcorn
and a coke
Jukebox, corner booth
and a dog
TV tuned to weather.
If you recall
this short report
then you've been to any
lakeside resort.

Ain't no sexy harmonica player

I wish I knew for sure
that the world was round
so I wouldn't have to travel
far
to trace the ground.
I wish I understood
the stars above
so I wouldn't have to spend
a dime
to contact love.
What's with the big blue sky
and a yellow sun
turning a potluck future
into one
dish.
Who owns the copyright
to color
and who decides
one love for another.
Why would a river overflow with tears
from one lonely song
that still lives on.
A tune as ancient as the earth
keeps rhythm to let us know
we're not the first
to ponder this
let every reed willing
blow!

Where I Go

I don't smoke
in the house
Not even in my frigid corner of the world
Five steps from my workshop
is the door.

I have a nest
It's in a small corner of the basement
where I house all the things that define me
My woodworking tools, my art stuff
my typewriter and the washing machine
Oh, how did that get there?
I meant
my power tools and small stereo
my many papers and books
my out takes on life.

Back to what I was saying
I don't smoke in the house
Instead, I sit on a wood step
through the door
connecting the garage
staring at my reflection
in the passenger window of the car
only ten inches from my knees
that's where I see myself the most
That's where I hear myself the most
Probably, that's where God hears me the most

On that cold hard wooden stoop
facing me and my problems, face to face
My best friend is the one who smiles
my enemy is the twisted angry me
At times, I've beaten the side of that car
no real reason, just , it was there.
And I've lingered way beyond a smoke
sitting on that stoop uncovering injustices
I could tell you the make of the tires
and the situation of the trim
every centimeter of rust that has come in
This is my place
I smoke here
I think here
I pray here
I am here.
It's cold and hard and average
but I get more out of my life being in this solace
then I ever do in my cozy bed.
Where we go to think, where we go to pray
these are the places of the heart
these are the places of our Lord.

While You Sleep
(A tribute to Edgar)

Candles burning
flickering light
Dancing shadows
box the night
Black cat wails
from a distant alley
Whistling winds
careen the valley
A full moon rises
over the shed
They move in circles
calling the dead
Dressed in robes
they break the crest
Willing souls
they put to rest
Storm clouds gather
whirling mist
Satan hurls
an angry fist
night is passing
soon dawn will come
Tracks are covered
the deed is done.

Just a Thought

What's that we find
in a poet's mind
In a poets mind
we find, what?
Where from this
rhyming, rythmic, rhetoric?
Where for and why and how?
Blessed are they
who paint with words?
Whose words are painted thoughts
in knots!
Makes me wonder
if I too a poet?
For my life seems
rhyming, rhetoric!

As far as I can tell

The turtle is not a social fella,

he crawls inside his shell.

But the lion, he's a boisterous one,

he'll stand right up and yell!

The trick in life,

it seems to me,

or -

as far as I can tell,

Stay somewhere between

the two extremes,

you may live long and well!

For What It's Worth

Here in my castle
just me and my keep
thoughts of my homeland
begin to seep
The years and the miles
have gotten me here
a crown with no jewels
a conscience I fear
Atop of my mountain
lord of all I survey
stands the loneliest one
of all I would say
With honor and pride
I stand alone
wishing my castle
would feel like a home
I got what I wanted
I shouldn't complain
I've got my kingdom
I've got my fame
Still -
I'd trade it all
for just one truth
You can have my kingdom
if I can have my youth.

My moments   My memories

The joy of my youth
was fresh and simple
Autumn being my favorite
Musky, colorful and brisk
it led to frigid and pure
covering all
It toughened skin and
souls as well
to live as nature
treated us
Spring collapsed the spoiled
rotting smell of hibernation
and threw so many green
and tender buds
how could anyone not know, breathe
love!
Summer sent my spirit
on vacation
no rules no logic
only swimming in sun
These are my moments, my memories
of earth as joy
to live within.

Swim

Jump in
feel the cool,
relax in the pleasure
a buoyed treasure.
The womb comes alive
to embrace you again
as when you began
your journey.
Swim free of the shore
yet never ignore
the distance.
Faith will carry your spirit
but the tide may take you out.
Always respect
the undercurrent
-as ugly as it is-
save your breath
pace your strokes
yet remember how to live.

If ever the water
seems too deep
or you fear
you're swimming alone,
call on me
I'll help you see
the light in the distance
is home!

ISBN 1553957199-9

9 781553 957195